ROLLS-ROYCE
& BENTLEY
CLASSIC ELEGANCE

PAUL W. COCKERHAM

TODTRI

This book was designed and produced by
TODTRI Book Publishers
P.O. Box 572, New York, NY 10116-0572
FAX: (212) 695-6984
e-mail: info@todtri.com

Printed and bound in Singapore

ISBN 1-57717-123-3

Author: Paul W. Cockerham

Publisher: Robert M. Tod
Senior Editor: Edward Douglas
Photo Editor: Linda Waldman
Designer: Mark Weinberg
Typesetting: Command-O, NYC

Visit us on the web!
www.todtri.com

Photo Credits

AUTOMOBILE QUARTERLY
4-5, 7, 8-9, 10 (top & bottom), 11, 12, 14 (top & bottom), 15, 17, 18, 19 (bottom),
20 (top & bottom), 21, 22 (bottom), 23, 24-25, 26, 28, 29, 30 (bottom left), 32 (top & bottom),
33, 34, 35, 36 (top & bottom), 37 (top & bottom), 38, 39 (top & bottom), 40-41, 42, 43, 44, 45, 46,
47, 48, 49, 50 (top), 51, 52, 54 (bottom), 55, 58 (top & bottom), 62, 63 (top & bottom), 64 (top & bottom),
67 (right), 68 (left), 70 (top left & bottom), 71 (top & right bottom), 72-73, 74, 75, back cover

RON KIMBALL
6, 16, 19 (top), 22 (top & middle), 27, 53, 54 (top), 56-57, 59, 60-61, 65, 66, 67 (left), 76-77, 78-79

JOHN LAMM
30-31 (top right & top), 31 (bottom), 50 (bottom), 68 (right), 69

Contents

Introduction

4

CHAPTER ONE

Beginnings

13

CHAPTER TWO

Shared Elegance

45

CHAPTER THREE

Divergence

68

Index

80

Introduction

If character and exclusivity are the qualities by which you judge automobiles, then it's hard to beat the creations of Rolls–Royce and Bentley. Given that the companies had a shared history that spanned more than fifty years, this should not seem so surprising.

Mottos for both makers reveal lofty aspirations. The Rolls–Royce was proclaimed to be (and few doubt it to be) "The Best Car in the World." Bentley was content to settle with "The Silent Sports Car," though few of its recent creations could be considered sports cars in the traditional sense.

To understand these two companies we need to become familiar with some background on personalities, and what they brought to their respective companies.

Henry Royce was a miller's son, born in 1863 near Petersborough, England. His father died when he was nine years old, and he was forced to sell newspapers in London to support his mother and aunt. He started apprenticing as a telegraph boy at the age of 12, and then took an apprenticeship with the Great Northern Railway. Money problems prevented him from completing this apprenticeship, however, and he started to take whatever jobs were available in the engineering and electrical fields. He had succeeded in schooling himself by this time, having taught himself algebra, several foreign languages, and engineering principals.

He showed a particular aptitude for engineering, and ultimately established his own firm on Cooke Street in Manchester. He was caught up in England's budding enthusiasm for motoring and bought his first car, a Decauville, in 1902. He had soon torn it down and rebuilt it to his own highly meticulous standards, which ultimately led him to construct his own car, superior to any offered at the time, in terms of engineering. This was the first Royce automobile.

Charles Stewart Rolls, third son of Lord and Lady Llangattock, was born in 1877, brought up on the family estate in Monmouthshire, attended Eton, and visited France

A 1924 Silver Ghost Boattail Speedster. This was the final year of production for the Silver Ghost.

When new, the 3.5–liter Bentley was purchased by many sports car fans, among them Woolf Barnato, Capt. George Eyston and Malcolm Campbell. The latter pair were world land speed record holders at various times. This is a 1935 drophead coupe.

at the age of 17, where he bought his first automobile, a Peugeot. Rolls was one of England's earliest car enthusiasts and did much to further the popularity of automobile racing there.

Rolls also had his enthusiasms for ballooning and aviation, and ultimately became a renowned flier, but it was in the automotive realm where he truly made his mark. He established a showroom in Mayfair and a nearby shop in Fulham, where he respectively sold the very best cars, such as Peugeots and Panhards. His path crossed with that of Royce in 1904 at a meeting in the Midland Hotel in Manchester, and it was that meeting that ultimately led to the formulation of Rolls–Royce.

Walter Owen (W. O.) Bentley, like Royce, was a railway engineering apprentice, but as his father was a London businessman, he was able to complete his

training. His passions included cricket and racing motorcycles, and he bought his first car in 1910, a Riley V–twin two–seater. By 1912, he had joined his brother H. M. Bentley in selling French DFP autos. W. O. created special aluminum/copper alloy pistons to boost their sluggish performance, and, thus equipped, the cars won several races at Brooklands during 1913–14.

He worked on the Royal Navy's Technical Board during the First World War, and returned to Bentley & Bentley after the conflict. His long–held vision to see a car bearing his own name was finally realized in August 1919, when he formed Bentley Motors Ltd.

The two companies maintained separate histories for several years, with Rolls–Royce building "bespoke" luxury automobiles of the highest engineering standards, and Bentley creating fast tourers and closed–bodied cars, along with a series of phenomenally successful racing cars.

But Bentley's production numbers were always small and the company was undercapitalized from the beginning, and by 1925 a majority interest had been sold to millionaire sportsman Woolf Barnato. A new model, the 8 liter, and the Depression's impact on Barnato's fortunes forced the company into receiver-ship. W. O. had had discussions with Napier about a new sports car and it was believed Napier would be the company, but the winning bid was fronted by a mysterious outfit called British Equitable Trust Ltd.; it was only a few days before the sale that W. O.'s wife heard, via cocktail party conversation, that this company was acting on behalf of Rolls–Royce.

Thus was Bentley Motors Ltd. formed in 1931 as a Rolls–Royce subsidiary. W. O. stayed on, but having little influence on vehicular development, left for Lagonda in 1935.

A 1909 Silver Ghost Landaulette, from the D. Cameron Peck collection. Note the filigree on the roof–mounted luggage rack.

FOLLOWING PAGE: Rolls–Royce's role in the development of the 3.5–liter Bentley gave it an oblique entrance into the world of motor sport. Cars such as this Sedanca Coupe by Owen, however, were for more of a sedate crowd, one would feel.

*"The Spirit of Ecstasy"
sculpture found on
the hood of Rolls–Royce
automobiles was created
in 1910 by Charles Sykes
after he had ridden in a
Silver Ghost. Its intricate
detail is created through
the lost wax process.*

The first new Bentley under Rolls–Royce's aegis, the 3.5 liter, was introduced in 1933, and was fitted with a modified Rolls–Royce 20/25 engine. Thereafter, Bentleys became increasingly similar to the offerings of the parent company, particularly after the Second World War when they shared production facilities at Crewe.

During this period, there was little to differentiate the two lines of cars, aside from hood ornamentation (Rolls–Royce's famed "Winged Ecstasy"; Bentley's winged "B") and the shape of radiators (the Bentley having a more rounded profile). This remained true through the early 1980s, when Bentley introduced the high–performance Mulsanne Turbo to give the line more of a sporting nature, a tendency further developed in subsequent models.

Rolls–Royce Motor Cars Ltd. had for years been a division of Rolls–Royce, which had become a major influence in gas turbine production and one of the world's leading purveyors of aircraft engines. The auto group was put on the block in the mid–1990s, and a spirited bidding war broke out between German automakers BMW AG and Volkswagen AG. Volkswagen stunned most

*John Paul Stack's 3–liter
"Red Label" Bentley.
The badge color refer-
ence signifies this car
as having a 9 foot, 9.5
inch wheelbase, and a
5.3:1 compression ratio.*

observers by winning this battle, and then stunned itself when it discovered
its purchase did not include rights to produce automobiles under the Rolls–
Royce name, rights that BMW ultimately purchased and will be able to
exercise as of the year 2003. Somewhat embarassed, Volkswagen has already
put its considerable engineering expertise to develop new engines and platforms for Bentley.

BMW, meanwhile, adds "The Best Car in the World" to its portfolio of
British automobile manufacturers, which also includes Rover.

In any event, Rolls–Royce and Bentley automobiles are no longer a province
of the British. Future products may well prove spectacular, but something of
their historical essence will be missing.

*A top view of a 1937
Rolls–Royce boattail
skiff. Note the separate
windscreen for the pas-
senger compartment.*

This 1914 Silver Ghost skiff is so named for
its lovely wooden boattail body. Its inline
six-cylinder engine was the first practical
application of such an engine in an autombile.

CHAPTER ONE

Beginnings

After their hotel meeting, Charles Rolls tried Henry Royce's car and pronounced the engineer "the man I had been looking for for years." The pair hammered out an agreement giving Rolls exclusive sales rights for every car Royce could produce. A variety of designs were created for the Paris Salon of 1904: a 10 hp car, a 10 hp engine and chassis, a 15 hp engine and chassis, a 20 hp car, and a 30 hp, six–cylinder engin—an ambitious debut for a company with no commercial experience. The pair celebrated Christmas a little early that year with the December 23 signing of a contract designating the fruits of their venture "Rolls–Royce."

Sadly, Charles Rolls had only a few years to enjoy his role as automotive manufacturer, as he was killed in a flying accident at Bournemouth on July 12, 1910. Henry Royce would continue to have an impact on daily operations at the company right until his death on April 22, 1933.

Early Successes and Failures

The inclusion of the 10 hp car in the initial product line was indicative of Royce's engineering genius. It was powered by a two–cylinder engine, which Rolls felt would be rough–running, like other such units of the time. It proved to be as smooth as larger, multiple–cylinder engines, thanks to a three–bearing crankshaft and improved lubrication. The new car also sported a radiator of classic Grecian shape that would become a trademark, as well as a logo of two entwined Rs.

The Rolls–Royce 15 hp was only in production from 1904–05; six cars were made. The engine did not run smoothly enough, and its problems were hard to resolve because it did not share the standard layout of the other engines. Part of the problem was due to Royce's insistence that the cars meet exacting quality and testing standards, which often created a situation throughout the company's history of never being able to produce enough models to meet demand.

The 20 hp and 30 hp models met the demands of Rolls' clientele for more powerful models, with the latter being the first six–cylinder car offered by the entire automotive industry. The 20 hp exactly matched the requirements of the Tourist Trophy race, having space for four passengers and specific weight and consumption requirements. Charles Rolls entered a 20 hp for himself in 1905, but he managed to ruin his gearbox early in the proceedings. Rolls recognized some improvements which Royce implemented: lighter alloy chassis and wheel components, and a new four–speed overdrive transmission were ready for 1906's event. Two cars were entered, one for Rolls and the other for Percy Northey. Northey bent his front axle when he hit a bridge, but Rolls won the event at an average speed 4 mph greater that his nearest competitor.

The company's marketing man, C. G. Johnson, persuaded Royce to create a new model for 1905 called the Legalimit, which boasted an extremely modern (for the time) V–8 engine. Designed to be as silent as an electrically powered car, the car got its name from a sophisticated gearbox design that restricted its top speed to the then–legal speed limit of the time, 20 mph. Frankly, ew customers were interested in obeying this absurd restriction, and there was never a market for the car. Only three Legalimits were made, none survive today.

A 1922 Silver Ghost with a rakish tourer body. The cars were known to be hugely reliable, and more than 7,800 were built.

The Silver Ghost

One of the endearing classics in all of motoring: a 1907 Silver Ghost, in silver. Solidly built, Silver Ghosts also saw duty as trucks, ambulances, and armored vehicles.

Capacity problems at the Cooke Street factory in Manchester were proving to be unsolvable, so Royce designed a new factory that was constructed through 1906–07 in the town of Derby. It was here that the company's first signature car was created, a creation first known as the Rolls–Royce 40/50 hp, but later came to be known as the Silver Ghost. Its six–cylinder, 7.0–liter engine was the first practical application of a straight six in an automobile. Its crankshaft rotated on seven main bearings, providing incredible smoothness, and pressure lubrication, a feature first introduced on the Legalimit, was utilized.

*An early Silver Ghost from 1907. Rolls–Royce created
a new factory in Derby for construction of the car.*

Work in the new factory was dedicated exclusively to the Silver Ghost; all other work ceased. By the time production ended in 1924, more that 6,173 of the hand–built cars had been produced, and the marque's reputation was solidly established.

Pinstriping, tufted seats, and intricate folding tops, such as those found on this Silver Ghost, were all part of the coachbuilder's art; integrating these talents has been a Rolls–Royce tradition from the beginning.

The car's reputation carried overseas as well, particularly in the United States. The company had agents in the country, but decided it needed a separate production facility as well, and such a facility was opened in Springfield, Massachusetts in 1921. Initially dedicated to final assembly of English–built Silver Ghosts, the plant was soon assembling its own cars, and managed to produce 1,703 vehicles before the car was discontinued in 1926.

A rear view of the 1924 Silver Ghost Boattail Speedster, showing off the wooden coachwork that gave it its name.

Quite racy looking is this 1928 Phantom I Blackhawk. A 7.7–liter inline six, good for 100 hp, powered this successor to the Silver Ghost.

Enter the Phantom

Though continuously improved, the design of the Silver Ghost had aged, and after the 20 hp was launched resources were dedicated to developing a successor. The New Phantom, ultimately known as the Phantom I, bowed in May 1925.

Its chassis was basically identical to that of its predecessor, albeit available in two wheelbase lengths: 143.25 inches and 150 1.2 inches. It had the same servo–assisted four–wheel brakes that had been built into the final generation of Silver Ghosts, and was powered by a 7.7–liter inline six.

The car sold well in an increasingly crowded market that included Bentley, Sunbeam, Daimler, and American makers Packard, Cadillac, and Lincoln. The engine's cast–iron head was ultimately replaced by an aluminum head to increase performance, and although the company never published (or publishes) performance figures for its cars, the engine was said to be good for 100 hp and stout enough to withstand the addition of a supercharger for those wanting more performance. The Phantom I remained in production both in England and America through 1931.

A 1928 Phantom I tourer. With left–hand drive and bodywork by Brewster & Co. of New York, this almost certainly was an American–built Rolls–Royce, constructed at the Springfield, Massachusetts factory.

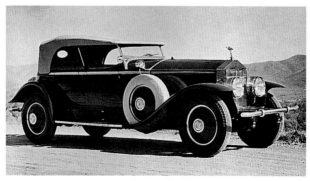

A 1925 Rolls–Royce Phantom I four–door tourer. The car remained in production both in England and America through 1931.

Brewster & Co. was apparently influenced by Art Deco design themes in creating this 1931 Phantom I "windblown" coupe.

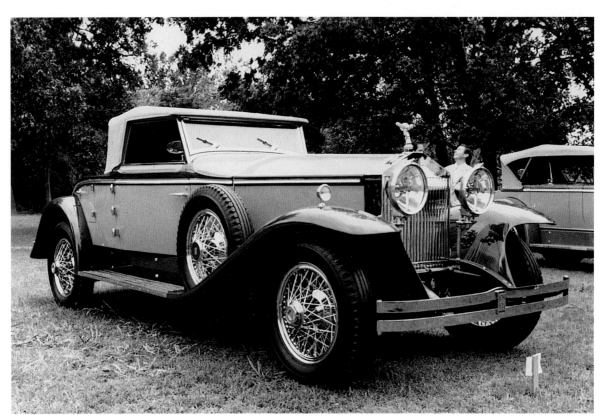

A 1931 Springfield–built Phantom I roadster, with bodywork by Brewster & Co. The American penchant for chrome trim is evident here.

Very much at home in stately surroundings is this 1930 Phantom I town convertible. The car sold well in an increasingly crowded market, which included Bentley, Sunbeam, Daimler, Packard, Cadillac, and Lincoln.

The Rolls–Royce Phantom II bowed in 1929 at London's Olympia Motor Show. Underslung springs and a lower frame helped emphasize the car's sleek lines.

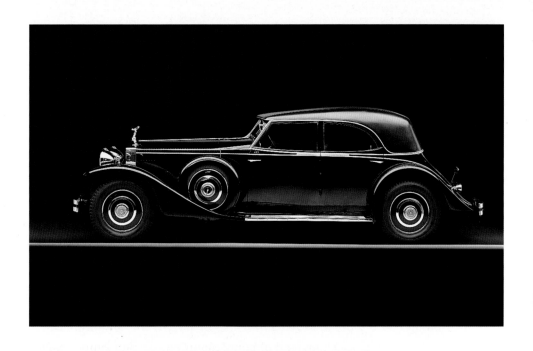

A study in elegance is this black, four–door Phantom II saloon from 1933. It remains one of Rolls–Royce's most classic designs.

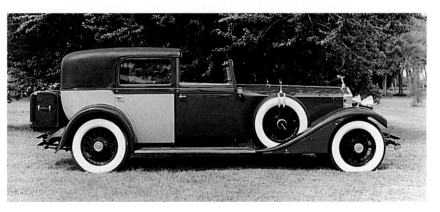

This 1930 Rolls–Royce Phantom II Brougham de Ville has bodywork by the legendary Hooper concern, which still does custom work to this day.

The big cars that followed, the Phantom II and Phantom II Continental, rank among the company's most classic, elegant designs. The Phantom II officially bowed at the London Olympia Motor Show of October 1929. Initially, the engine was basically unchanged, save for the use of an aluminum cylinder head, but some up–to–date alterations were found in the chassis. Both axles now had half–eliptical springs. These were underslung in the rear axle, and combining this with a lower frame created a car with considerably reduced height. The engine, clutch, and gearbox were combined into one unit and bolted directly to the chassis, instead of being mounted to a subframe. Inside, gauges and dials had been updated.

It was here that the company really started getting coy about performance figures. It was cultivating an image as a producer of faultlessly reliable, elegant cars with perfect driving manners, so it didn't really aspire to compete, in terms of sheer horsepower, with competitors of the time. Still, a sporty model, wearing a sports saloon body, was developed, at Royce's insistence and over the objections of the sales department. After being shown at a fashionable Concours d'Elegance in Biarritz, and after a demonstration run through France and Spain, the car returned home to find that the sales department had designated it the Phantom II Continental and had already produced sales brochures.

This is a 1932 Phantom II two–door convertible. An aluminum cylinder head and half–eliptical springs added to the car's sporting appeal.

FOLLOWING PAGE: A side view of a 1932 Rolls–Royce Phantom II convertible. The compartment door in front of the rear wheel is for the stowage of golf clubs.

Most stately is this lovely gray 1936 Phantom III. Its light alloy engine block displaced 7.3 liters and was inaudible at speed.

The new Rolls–Royce Phantom III, introduced in October 1935, joined the ranks of 12–cylinder luxury cars available from other makers. The car was virtually inaudible at speed and devoid of vibration, and seemed totally ignorant of its size and bulk as it accelerated to speed. Its light alloy engine block displaced 7.3 liters, and the engine and gearbox were mounted on rubber to minimize vibration. It was a unique car for the time, made from the best, most costly materials throughout. It also featured an independent front suspension, which required less space and allowed designers to allocate more space to the engine compartment.

The big engine, the car's major attraction, proved to be its undoing. Autobahn–traveling Europeans, running the car at top speed for extended periods, were inducing heat–related failures. A higher fourth gear helped, but the car's reputation by then had been damaged, and only 727 Phantom IIIs were constructed.

This 1936 Rolls–Royce Phantom III two–door saloon was subjected to some rather extreme bodywork. The car was the company's first V–12–powered auto.

Get Small

A smaller car, developed from 1919 to 1922, was the foundation of the company's success in the twenties. Also known as the 20 hp (this was a tax designation; output from its 3–liter engine was 53 hp), it was a smaller car that the company created for a market interested in driving itself about, rather that being chauffeured. It also became the vehicle through which the company convinced coachbuilders to produce bodies of a scale, strength, and weight more appropriate to motoring. It's radiator shutters were arranged horizontally and were controlled by the driver, giving it a distinct appearance. (They were changed back to the traditional vertical orientation during its last year of production, 1929.) With 2,885 units produced, it was a very successful automobile indeed.

A successor to the 20 hp came about in 1929 with the introduction of the 20/25 hp. The engine was boosted to 3.7 liters, and compression increased to 4.6:1, making for more usable power. The car's incredible power band remained the same, meaning that it could be put into top gear soon after starting and left there. The chassis design saw continual improvements, including, after 1932, the fitting of modified shock absorbers to improve passenger comfort and roadhandling. Adjustable units were fitted two years later.

Sales for the model reached 3,827, making it Rolls–Royce's best–selling car between the wars. It in turn was succeeded by the 25/30 hp of 1936–38 as the company's "small" car. This, in turn, was succeeded by the first small Rolls–Royce with a name: the Wraith.

The Wraith was a very modern motorcar with a totally welded chassis and independent fronts suspension, like the Phantom III. It had smaller wheels with balloon tires, giving it a softer ride. A new, cross–flow cylinder head allowed the 4.3–liter engine to be run at high revs for quite awhile, something its big brother couldn't always claim. A truly neat new feature was integrated road jacks, hydraulically powered, mounted at each axle.

A 1937 Rolls–Royce 25/30 skiff type roadster. This type of bodystyle was popular with rich young dilletantes of the time.

Rolls–Royce produced the 20/25 for customers to drive themselves, rather than as a chauffeur–driven vehicle. This was the company's best–selling car between the wars.

Bentley Rising

W. O's most valued asset as his company launched was Frank Burgess, who had been a designer and works driver for Humber. Burgess brought over a Tourist Trophy Humber to Bentley Motors, which was quick to incorporate some of its chassis features into the new car.

Burgess' ideas for engine design were radical for the era. It had only a single camshaft, driven off the crankshaft by a vertical connecting shaft at the front of the four–cylinder, inline engine. It had four valves per cylinder, with a long bore and stroke of 80mm x 149mm. It displaced 2,996 cc and thus provided the car with the designation of the 3–liter model, a confusing nomenclature to British motorists accustomed to hp ratings of the time. The car had a four–speed gearbox activated by an external handgear lever on the right side, four–wheel, semi–eliptical leaf springs, and brakes only on the rear wheels (until 1924, that is). The first car, a two–door saloon, was delivered in September 1921 at a price of £1,150 ($5,750), and soon a two–year waiting list had developed.

The company was soon very successful, compiling many high–profile victories at the race track while attracting customers such as Prince George, Gertrude Lawrence, and Beatrice Lillie.

The company did not have its own coachworks, so it made some standard recommendations for the time, particularly four–seated open tourers made by

One of the prettiest, most exotic Bentleys you'll ever see is this 1925 3–liter torpedo tourer with coachwork by Viotti of Torino, Italy.

A 1926 Bentley 3 liter, no doubt used for competition. It had a four-speed gearbox and semi-eliptical leaf springs. Brakes were on the rear wheels only until 1924.

The 3-liter engine that gave the Bentley 3 liter its name. It had four valves per cylinder and a single camshaft, driven off the crankshaft by a vertical connecting shaft at the front of the engine.

Setting a sporty note is this 1928 Bentley Speed Six with a torpedo body. Its radiator had parallel sides, compared to that of the 6 1/2, which tapered toward the bottom.

This 1928 Bentley 6.6–liter has a four–door saloon body by Gurney–Nutting. A heavy car with high running speeds, the 6.5 created problems for tires with regularity.

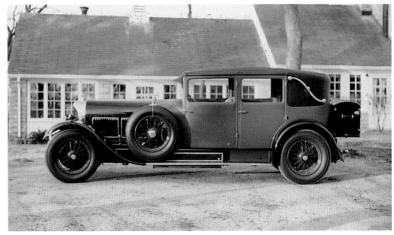

Vanden Plas, headquartered nearby. Other makers soon got in the act, providing everything from two–seaters to landaulettes. Bentley saw his cars primarily as fast tourers, but realized that more power would be needed to satisfy the demands of coachbuilders and customers. His first inclination was a six–cylinder unit based on the existing 3 liter, but after seeing the Rolls–Royce Phantom I in France, W. O. opted in favor of displacement, and created a six–cylinder engine displacing 6.6 liters. The engine's design differed primarily from the 3 liter by having a three–throw coupled rod instead of a vertical shaft.

The new chassis featured a cone clutch instead of a plate clutch, it had a much heavier differential, and four–wheel, finned drum brakes. As the 6.5, it catered quite well to the luxury market.

The sporting version, unveiled in 1928, was known as the Speed Six. This car was Bentley's most successful racing model, as it enjoyed two consecutive wins at LeMans (in 1928 and 1929). It also wore formal coachwork.

A 1928 Bentley 3–liter sports model. The matte finish on the side of the car indicates doped cloth bodywork, often used on racing models.

The 1930 Blue Train Bentley Speed Six at rest.
Speed Sixes were the company's most successful racing
model, having two consecutive wins at LeMans.

*This 1930 Bentley Speed Six is also known as
the Blue Train Bentley, as it defeated a fast
express during a record overland run in the 1930s.*

This Bentley 4.5 two-door open tourer is from 1928. All told, 665 of the cars were built, including 55 Blower Bentleys.

Sir Henry Birkin, one of the "Bentley Boys", driving the 4.5-liter Blower Bentley at the 1930 French Grand Prix, where he finished second.

Bentley wanted a new sports car to stay competitive in the late twenties, and developed the 4.5 as an answer. Dimensionally the same size as the 6.5 but using many of the components from the 3 liter, it was most popular with customers, to W. O.'s regret, with a longer wheelbase option. Supercharged racing versions, known as the "Blower Bentleys", were good for 240 hp, but never proved particularly reliable in competition.

As far as Bentley was considered, when in doubt, make the engine larger, and W. O. preferred developing a new, big mill as opposed to supercharging

A 1930 4.5–liter "Blower" Bentley. The company preferred to boost performance through larger engines, rather than by supercharging, which they thought to be unreliable.

A 1929 Bentley 4.5 open tourer. When production started at the end of 1927, the cars were built in batches of 25 at a time, with minor modifications being incorporated along the way.

This Murphy-bodied Bentley 8-liter roadster could easily reach 100 mph. It was tough finding a market for the car during the Depression Era, and Bentley was soon in receivership.

a smaller engine. Thus was the case with the 8 liter, essentially the 6.5 bored and stroked to a capacity of 7, 982cc. Depending on the compression ratio, output could be either 200 hp or 225 hp It could be had in two wheelbases, the longer reaching an amazing 13 feet. With a light enough body fitted, the car could still exceed 100 mph

Introduction timing for the new car, however, proved disastrous, particularly with the Depression in full flower. Few wanted to buy expensive cars, and only 67 of the 100 8-liter chassis had been sold by the time Bentley found itself consumed by Rolls-Royce in 1931.

The Joint Venture Begins

The initial impression from the joint venture was that Bentley's sporting reputation would be maintained, as the new 3.5 liter introduced in 1933, with a higher compression ratio, produced 105 hp, 20 more than its sister 20/25 variant from Rolls-Royce. Only chassis were supplied, with sports tourer bodies suggested from Vanden Plas and four-door saloons from Park Ward.

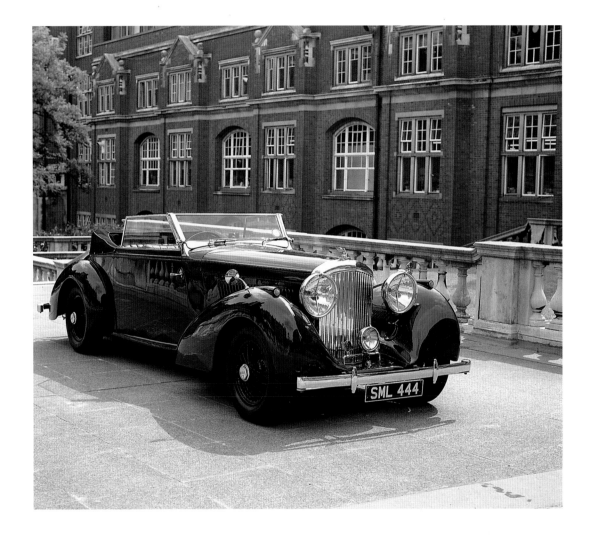

FOLLOWING PAGE: *W. O. Bentley envisioned his cars as fast tourers, which is what this 1929 Speed Six roadster exemplifies.*

The engine in the 3.5–liter Bentley was based on Rolls–Royce's 20/25 unit, which took to the performance modifications with ease. This is another view of the 1935 drophead coupe.

The 3.5–liter Bentley met public demand for a powerful automobile of exceptional handling. The Sedanca Coupe body in this 1934 model is by Owen.

It was the smoothest, most comfortable Bentley to date, and even W. O. noted that "Taking all things into consideration, I would rather own this Bentley than any car produced under that name."

Heavier coachwork soon spurred the development of a 4.25– liter variant, which was introduced in 1936. This was good for about 16 additional hp. Production reached 1,241 cars.

The Mark V was the final prewar Bentley, using many front suspension and transmission bits from the Rolls–Royce Wraith. It was introduced in the summer of 1939 and probably no more than 20 units had been produced before the war brought production to a close. One unit was the basis for a beautiful, streamlined saloon known as the Bentley Corniche. Designed by M. G. Paulin and built by Van Vooren of Paris, it had engine and suspension updates as well as a slick body. The single prototype, unfortunately, was damaged during a traffic accident in France. The body was shipped back to England for repair but was destroyed in an air raid during the war.

A classic, four–seater, open–touring Bentley, probably a 1930 4.5 model, in the style of coach-builder Vanden Plas.

A 1933 Bentley 3.5–liter drophead coupe. Many of the first bodies were built as cabriolets, but closed versions were soon available, primarily by Park Ward.

Roughly one–fifth of the 5,200 Bentley Mark VIs received individual coachwork, as was the case with this 1947 drophead coupe.

CHAPTER TWO

Shared Elegance

After the war, all Bentleys and Rolls–Royces were assembled together at the factory at Crewe, which during the war had built aircraft engines.

When the new Mark VI Bentley appeared in 1946, it was the first time that the company had produced a complete car: chassis, engine, and bodywork. Coachwork was produced outside the facility at Pressed Steel's factory and the shell delivered to Crewe, where the company's new staff of exterior painters, upholsterers and cabinet makers did their duty, and to what turned out to be a very high standard.

Body lines of the car recalled the prewar Park Ward saloons, although headlights were integrated into the front fenders. The chassis was fitted with the 4.25–liter B60 engine, now boasting an aluminum cylinder head, a camshaft with higher lift and twin SU carburators. Approximately 5,200 Mark VIs were produced during its six–year production run.

Its sister car was Rolls–Royce's Silver Wraith, which still was available only as a rolling chassis. Mechanically the same as the Bentley in all major respects, its engine had different

A Rolls–Royce Silver Wraith from 1950. A sister car to the
Mark VI Bentley, it was fitted with a 4 1/4–liter inline six.

carburators that provided greater torque but less power than that found in the Mark VI. Increased bore produced a larger, 4.5–liter engine for both cars in 1951. The same year a longer, 133–inch wheelbase chassis, which delighted coachbuilders, was unveiled for the Silver Wraith.

Still, these were hard times in which to sell a Rolls. Former British colonies were becoming independent (no more mass sales of Rolls–Royces to Indian rahjahs, for example), taxes were high to finance reconstruction, and gas rationing was still in place. Only 1,783 examples of the Silver Wraith were produced from 1946–59.

A 1947 Bentley Mark VI drophead coupe. The Mark VI became the most successful Bentley that Rolls–Royce ever built.

A 1951 Bentley Mark VI Coupe de Ville. Engine
capacity grew from 4.2 liters to 4.6 liters that year.

Rolls–Royce targeted the American market when it introduced the V–8 powered Silver Dawn in 1949. Sales were hurt by the car's having a manual shifter. This is a 1953 model.

The Silver Dawn

These social and political realities played a large role in the introduction of Rolls–Royce's Silver Dawn in 1949. Squarely aimed at the American market, if the car were successful it would help the company meet a governmental requirement and gain access to raw materials in the home market. Basically a left–drive, badge–engineered Mark VI Bentley, it had limited initial success because it was solely equipped with a column–mounted, four–speed, manual shifter. The market was used to automatic transmissions, but it wasn't until 1952 that one was offered by Bentley, in the form of General Motors' Hydramatic unit.

Unfortunately, both this car and the Mark VI, the company's initial attempts at producing complete automobiles, were highly susceptible to rust. The company did not fully understand the precautions necessary to prevent body rot, and the quality of raw materials available at the end of the war was questionable to begin with. As such, the ones seen today have usually benefited from considerable, expensive restoration.

Return of the Phantom

The Rolls–Royce Phantom IV had a somewhat tortured evolution. The company had vowed never to build any more cars in the "big" Phantom series after the war ended, but in 1950 an order came in to build a state limousine for HRH The Princess Elizabeth and HRH Prince Philip. Daimler had fallen out of favor with the royal family, and during the war the future Prince Philip had gotten his hands on "The Scalded Cat", an experimental Bentley in which Rolls–Royce was testing a new inline eight–cylinder engine, and he had become quite fond of it.

The company created the Phantom IV from the prototype. A long, massively strengthened Silver Wraith chassis with a wheelbase of 145 inches, overall length of 229.5 inches and width of 75.5 inches made for an immense vehicle, though one capable of speeds up to 100 mph. A partition noted this as a chauffeur–driven vehicle, although a special front seat was fitted for the occasions when Prince Philip wanted to drive.

The Phantom IV was the most exclusive Rolls–Royce ever built, with production limited to 18 vehicles, and delivery restricted to royalty and heads of state.

H. J. Mulliner bodied this 1955 Rolls–Royce Phantom IV limousine. This most exclusive Rolls saw only 18 examples made.

An extremely rare 1954
Bentley R Continental, with
body by Pininfarina. The
car was reputed to be the
fastest four-seater production
car in the world at the time.

A very advanced motor car was
the Bentley R Continental. This
(relatively) lightweight coupe
had a top speed of 117 mph
and could reach 60 mph in 14
seconds. This is a 1954 model.

Changing of the Guard

A new guard was taking over at Rolls–Royce, now a large concern with special sections devoted entirely to engine manufacture for vehicles and aircraft. Harry Grylls was now head of motor car production in a company where such activity had been relegated to a sideline. When it came time to create a successor to the Bentley Mark VI, he chose a conservative route.

The Bentley R, launched in 1952, wasn't a new car at all, but simply a stretched version of its predecessor. Eight inches longer than the Mark VI, the car now had an automatic choke, two–speed windshield wiper and heated rear lights as standard equipment. The nomenclature was new, to avoid confusion with the Mark series being produced by Jaguar.

It was a practical car, particularly with its larger trunk. Initially available with a four–speed manual, the R soon offered the GM Hydramatic box, which became standard equipment in 1954. The new unit could propel the R to a top speed of 107 mph.

A lightweight sports coupe based on the Mark VI was in the planning stages by 1950, and a sleek, low–drag body design was part of the plan from the beginning. Coachwork for the prototype was built by H. J. Mulliner, off a design featuring two doors, four seats and a small trunk (or "boot"). Wind tunnel tests put small fins on the rear fenders for directional stability; a redesigned exhaust gave the B80 engine an additional 25 hp.

Thus complete, the Bentley R Continental was introduced in 1952, and with a top speed of 117 mph for awhile held the position of fastest four–passenger sports car in the world. The first 100 cars were built exclusively for export; it was only thereafter it could be had domestically. Overall, 207 of the cars—most with Mulliner's sleek coupe body—were produced.

The Golden Gate Bridge provides a fitting backdrop for this 1954 Bentley R Continental. H. J. Mulliner built the coachwork for the prototype.

The Silver Cloud and Others

The next new product developments were announced by the company in April 1955. The Rolls–Royce Silver Cloud would replace the Silver Dawn, and the Bentley S would replace the R. For the first time, the two lines of cars would differ only in their radiators and badges.

J. P. Blatchley designed the base body, and his work on the Bentley R Continental showed through. Pressed Steel produced the body, which was attached to the still–separate and massive chassis at Crewe; doors, trunk, and hood lids were made of aluminum.

The engine was the 4.9–liter inline eight used in the R Continental. A new cylinder head allowed compression to be increased, a blessing because these "small" cars had become rather large.

The driver could choose between hard or soft shock absorber control by flicking a switch on the steering column. Triple–circuit drum brakes were found on all four wheels. Power steering was the most–requested option, so this was made standard from 1956–on.

Within six months of its introduction, the S received a Continental partner. The engine was tuned a bit, and tires of lower rolling resistance were fitted. A new rear axle ratio allowed the S Continental to reach 119 mph. Most of the 431 bodies for this car were built by H. J. Mulliner, which ultimately created a four–door coupe variant for the Continental chassis that it called the Flying Spur. Its low, sporty lines won it its own devoted following, and it was a much more athletic looking four–door than Rolls–Royce's own Standard Steel saloon.

The "Flying Spur" of H. J. Mulliner: a.k.a. the Bentley S2 Continental for 1962. Standard factory saloon bodies from Pressed Steel were stodgy by Mulliner's standards.

*This is a 1958 Rolls–Royce Silver Cloud I. Pressed Steel produced
the body, which was sent to the Crewe works for final assembly.*

The Rolls–Royce Silver Cloud II was fitted with the company's first V–8 engine, which had an alloy block and a gear–driven camshaft. This is a 1960 model.

Aside from the shape of the grill, there is nothing to distinguish this 1959 Bentley S1 from a Rolls–Royce Silver Cloud I of the same period.

The three cars in the line were very successful worldwide, and when their successors bowed in 1959, they were posthumously redesignated the Silver Cloud I and the S1.

The Silver Cloud II, S2 and S2 Continentals were almost impossible to distinguish from their predecessors, in terms of visual cues. But the company's engineers had been quite busy. A new V–8 engine was now under the hood. Its configuration allowed it to fit under the hood without expensive alteration to either chassis or body. The American market, too, had a predilection for V–8s.

The 6.2–liter, oversquare (cylinder bore is greater than stroke) had a light alloy block with wet steel cylinder liners. Its single camshaft was located in the center of the "vee" and gear driven, said to provide a longer life than a chain drive. The exhaust system was particularly quiet because each of its three mufflers was tuned to a certain range of frequencies.

This time around, the S2 Continentals were mechanically the same as the other cars, although, being fitted with all–aluminum bodies, their relative low weight gave them better acceleration numbers than the other models. In any case, 100 mph could now be reached in 38.5 seconds. The previous models needed an additional 12 seconds to reach this milestone. Top speed was in excess of 100 mph.

Seemingly resigned to its fate as a producer of large, chauffeur–driven vehicles, the company also announced in 1959 the new Rolls–Royce Phantom V, based on the Silver Cloud II. An idea of the intended market can be found in the fact that the GM Hydramatic was modified to provide a truly low final

Bodied by Young is this 1961 Rolls–Royce Phantom V. Based on the Silver Cloud II. It could cruise at a walking pace without complaint: perfect for ceremonial occasions.

FOLLOWING PAGE: A 1960 Silver Cloud II. Aside from the V–8 under the hood, the cars are impossible to distinguish from their predecessors.

This is a 1961 Rolls-Royce Phantom V, bodied by Young. Five hundred and sixteen of these specialized vehicles were produced—a respectable number.

A 1965 Bentley S3. Along with its sister, the Rolls-Royce Silver Cloud III, these were the company's last cars built with separate chassis and coachwork.

gear that allowed the car to progress without complaint at a walking pace—perhaps for ceremonial occasions. Overall production reached 516 vehicles, respectable given the specialized niche market involved.

When the next generation of cars were introduced in 1962, the Silver Cloud III, Bentley S3 and S3 Continental were interim models for the company. They were still built in a traditional manner, with separate coachwork and chassis being attached by screws and bolts, rather than using the unibody approach every other manufacturer had adopted by that time.

They still enjoyed some updates, primarily to the engine. Compression had been raised to 9:1, and another pair of carburators had been added which considerably boosted acceleration. A fully adjustable passenger's seat was now available, and greater leg and hip room was found in the rear.

Overall, the Silver Cloud/S series resulted in 13,000 standard cars being produced from 1955–65, with another 2,000 special–built cars using chassis. When the modern Silver Shadow was introduced, however, in 1965, it was more than a year before construction of the Silver Cloud/S ceased, as the company felt it couldn't turn its back on customers who wanted bodies built to their own specifications.

The Rolls–Royce Silver Cloud III enjoyed some engine modifications, including boosted compression and a second pair of SU carburators, which greatly benefited acceleration.

An imposing 1964 Rolls–Royce Silver Cloud III drophead coupe. The cars were still being built in the traditional manner, with separate chassis and coachwork being attached by screws and bolts.

A Bentley T from 1968, with coachwork by Pininfarina. At the time, oblong head-lamps were truly radical.

Suddenly, Modern Cars

Classic design and minute attention to detail had always marked Rolls-Royce as a manufacturer, with car development happening, it was perceived, only on an evolutionary footing. So the motoring world was fairly stunned when the Silver Shadow and Bentley T were unveiled in October 1965: these were thoroughly modern automobiles.

Ten years in the making, the cars used a monocoque chassis for the first time. The wheels were all now sprung independently, and stopping power was provided by four-wheel disk brakes.

J. P. Blatchley had done the design, and again, Pressed Steel provided the bodies, which were modern but made no concession to popular tastes. The wheelbase was shorter by 3.5 inches, and the overall length was 7.5 inches shorter; track and height were also reduced. Yet passenger and trunk space had increased.

The body provided a link between front and rear subframes. Road shocks were absorbed by coil springs and telescopic dampers at all four corners. The suspension could handle cruising in comfort as well as high-speed driving.

The three-circuit brake system was but one indication that the company was determined to become a leading force in automotive safety. Another was a steering system that had a kinked column that would not lance into the passenger compartment in an accident.

The engine was the same V-8 introduced in the Silver Cloud, now fitted with modified cylinder heads that optimized output by about 2 percent. Controls for the GM Hydramatic transmission were now electric, for ease of use.

The interior, as always, made judicious use of hides from Connolly Brothers, and featured a dashboard of walnut veneer, highly laquered. Instruments were now grouped in front of the driver.

The Phantom remained the pinnacle of the company's offerings, and this was reinforced when the Phantom VI rolled out, to somewhat skeptical notice, in 1968. The company had over time acquired the last two coachbuilders extant—Park Ward and H. J. Mulliner—and had created its own coachbuilding division around the two, based in Willesden in London and operating as Mulliner Park Ward. The company now had internalized all the resources needed to cater to the increasingly small, but still profitable, custom coachwork market.

The car was basically identical to the Phantom V, save for having the new twin headlamps of the Silver Shadow, as well as, more importantly, its new V-8 engine. A distinguishing feature was the use of two separate air conditioning systems: one for the chauffeur, the other for the passenger compartment.

A truly radical styling exercise was this 1963 Bentley Continenal convertible, with coachwork by Park Ward. The headlamps look vaguely Edselesque to this viewer.

The 1965 Bentley T was a truly modern car at its introduction, having monocoque construction, fully independent suspension and hydraulic disk brakes on all four wheels.

*Like any tra-
ditional British
convertible, this
Rolls–Royce
Corniche stacks
its folded top above
the deck and tucks
it under a cover.*

The Corniche

A truly stunning development was the introduction of the Corniche, two–
door coupes and cabriolets built at Mulliner Park Ward as an offshoot of the
Silver Shadow, in March 1971. The cars were relatively speedy, with modified
camshafts and a new exhaust system providing a power increase of 10 percent.
The top speed was in excess of 125 mph.

   The car became the starting point for the introduction of technical innova-
tions that found their way into other cars in the line. Ventilated disk brakes
and breakerless electronic ignition fall into this category.

*This Rolls–Royce
Corniche coupe looks
quite sporty under its
vinyl top. The cars were
relatively speedy, with
a new camshaft and
modified exhaust system
that boosted power 10
percent over that offered
by the Silver Shadow.*

*The Corniche was a
two–door coupe or cab-
riolet built at Millener
Park Ward as an off-
shoot of the Rolls–Royce
Silver Shadow. The
car could top 125 mph.*

A Corniche convertible, under the Brooklyn side of the Brooklyn Bridge in New York. The cars were the embodiment of cosmopolitan elegance.

For open–air touring at its finest, nothing makes quite a statement like this 1971 Rolls–Royce Corniche.

Divergence

Recent history for Rolls–Royce and Bentley grows from severe financial problems that troubled the aircraft engine division, problems that put the company into receivership in 1971 (it was ultimately acquired that year by Vickers).

The automotive division at this time, however, was in pretty good shape, largely because of the introduction of the Silver Shadow and Bentley T. They enjoyed splendid sales, and the receiver allowed the automotive division to carry on, with an eye towards spinning it off as a separate entity.

The Rolls–Royce Silver Shadow was the company's first truly modern automobile, having a monocoque chassis, independent suspension all around, and four–wheel disk brakes. This is a 1974 long–wheelbase sedan.

By 1997, Bentley had re–established its own reputation as a sporting marque, thanks to the spectacular popularity of cars such as this Turbo Continental R.

The automotive division's officers were all for this move. Confidently, they introduced a new range of cars in February 1977, consisting of the Rolls–Royce Silver Shadow II, Silver Wraith II and Bentley T2.

The cars were outwardly identifiable by bumpers with rubber inserts, to comply with U. S. regulations. Cars not bound for that country had a front air dam.

The sophisticated air conditioning system found in the Camargue provided automatic temperature control. For the driver, there was a new rack–and–pinion steering system that provided a crisper, more responsive feel, largely due to the retuned front suspension system. Speed control was found on the gear selection column.

The Silver Wraith II resurrected that name for the long–wheelbase model. It was four inches longer, all to the benefit of rear passenger legroom.

This line was in turn replaced by the Silver Spirit, the Silver Spur and Bentley Mulsanne of 1980. The designs were by Austrian stylist Fritz Feller, and although they looked longer than the offerings of the previous generation, exterior differences were small. A low waistline and emphasized horizontal lines made for a lower, leaner appearance.

Inside were the expected combinations of wood and leather, although now one could order high–grade velours for seating surfaces. A large center console extended from the front, where controls for the entertainment system, external mirrors and seats were kept, to the back. In the long–wheelbase Silver Spur, this extended to the back, where one could install office equipment, a video system with television, or a cocktail cabinet which could be refrigerated.

The fact that the Bentley was christened with a name (Mulsanne is the famous straight of the LeMans circuit) was the first indication that Bentley's profile was destined to rise, a deliberate move by the company's executives to support the carmaker as a whole.

If you were a Bentley fan during the post–war years, you had to be somewhat disappointed with Rolls–Royce's stewardship of the marque. Right after the war, the Mark VI outsold RR offerings by nearly three to one, but by the 1970s Bentley badges were found on only 10 percent of the company's output; that figure dropped to 4 percent by 1980.

Completely redesigned, the 1977 Bentley T2 had U.S.-mandated "5 mph" bumpers. new rack–and-pinion steering, speed control, and an emissions management system.

Only the radiator painted in the body's color signifies that this dignified saloon is, in reality, a snarling 1984 Bentley Mulsanne Turbo.

The Rolls–Royce Camargue was designed to highlight the company's technical advances, but the financial crisis of 1971 delayed its introduction. This is a 1975 model.

A high–performance Bentley was introduced in the spring of 1982 that launched the rebirth of the marque. The Mulsanne Turbo used a turbocharger from Garrett AiResearch that boosted horsepower 50 percent, from 200 to 300. A turbo boost limiter kept the top speed down to 135 mph, in line with car weight and tire limitations, but the modification meant the 2.5–ton car could accelerate from zero to 60 mph in only 7.5 seconds, an incredible feat. It was distinguished from the regular Mulsanne in that its radiator shell was painted the same color as its body.

Three years later an improved model bowed, the Turbo R, with beefed–up suspension bits and larger tires. Greater stiffness was brought to the anti–roll bars, as well as to limiting the play in the hydraulic self–leveling units in the rear.

The lineup was rounded out by a less–expensive Bentley, the Eight, which had a mesh grill and less–luxurious interior appointments.

These moves truly energized Bentley sales. By 1986, the group had sold 2,603 Bentleys, decreasing the RR/Bentley ratio to 60:40. Sales for group had slumped overall by 1991 to 1,731 cars, but fully 50 percent of these were Bentleys.

The Bentley trio was joined by a new model introduced at the 1991 Geneva Salon, the Continental R. An evocation of the R–type Continental of 35 years earlier, being a limited–production, high–performance, four–place, two–door coupe, one meant to sell at a premium. Designed by Ken Greenley and John Hefferman and based on a 1985 show car called Project 90, Engine output was increased to 333 hp, which was delivered through a GM four–speed automatic gearbox. A two–year waiting list materialized the day the car went on sale.

That the car was a success was no surprise, for Rolls–Royce had used meticulous market research for the first time in its history to see if demand existed for a two–door luxury sports coupe of aggressive appearance. Given that Rolls–Royce's own Phantom VI was destined to be discontinued later in 1991,

A 1975 Rolls–Royce Camargue coupe. The controversial body styling was by Pininfarina.

FOLLOWING PAGE: With the Mulsanne Turbo, Bentley had indeed returned to the sports car scene, albeit in a large-scale fashion. The car ducked many markets because of emissions regulations.

A dashboard shot of a 1975 Camargue two–door coupe. A walnut veneer dash, covered with many polished layers of clear lacquer, was a trademark.

Rolls–Royce interiors were always fitted with the finest leathers from Connolly Brothers. This is from a 1975 Camargue.

the company found that it now had a Bentley at the top of its model hierarchy. In terms of power, equipment, and price, it was clearly the company's top model.

The body color incorporated the radiator, bumpers, and exterior mirrors. Air ducts were found in the front bumper to cool the heat exchanger and front brakes. A winged "B" was cast onto the surface of the aluminum alloy wheels.

The Continental R's leather–trimmed seats were ergonomically shaped. Bucket seats were also found in the rear, divided by the single console that ran front to back. Inside were a centrally mounted gearshift lever, programmed seat controls, split–level air–conditioning controls, the entertainment system, and lockable storage areas.

The Continental R was motivated by the same turbocharged V–8 found in the Turbo R, but it used a new four–speed automatic that allowed the use of programmed sports or standard gear change patterns. Digital K–Motronic fuel injection and a microprocessor–controlled ignition system helped the car achieve zero–to–60 times in under 7 seconds, with a limited top speed of 145 mph. The car could reach its top speed at ease and was so well–built that the only sound heard in the interior was that of the rubber whirring over the pavement.

It was with the Continental R that Rolls–Royce succeeded in fully reviving the Bentley tradition of sporting coupes, but with build and quality characteristics that were distinctively that of Rolls–Royce.

The Eight and the Mulsanne S were replaced in September 1992 by a new car, the Brooklands. It featured aerodynamic body improvements, special alloy wheels, and inside, the gearchange lever was moved to the more sporting location on the floor.

Always There

With models coming and going around them over the years, the original two–door Rolls–Royce and Bentley Corniches had a remarkably long production run. Being the first to benefit from any technical improvement the company might develop no doubt extended their lifetime.

The Bentley Continental, introduced in 1984 as a replacement for the Bentley Corniche, had no significant technical differences from the Rolls–Royce Corniche. It had radiator slats that matched its exterior paint color, quite a distinguishing characteristic. Bumpers, rear–view mirrors, and tail-lights were slightly revised.

The Rolls–Royce Corniche II rolled out in 1988. Major revisions included the addition of anti–lock brakes, and a switch over to fuel injection. A new front suspension was also fitted. A wealth of minor modifications were found inside the car, including a central armbox capable of storage, the moving of analog switches to the central console, and the addition of memory seat position controls.

The Rolls–Royce Corniche III of 1989 was indistinguishable from the

aided delivery for the dual–level air–conditioning system. When the model went off–line in 1991, it brought to an end all production at Mulliner Park Ward's Willesden factory, and an age of coachbuilding elegance had truly come to an end.

Rolls–Royce introduced its new base models, the Silver Spirit II and the long–wheelbase Silver Spur II, in September 1989. At the time, there was speculation as to whether this particular line of cars had reached the end of the road, as it were, and whether a new series of cars would be released sometime in the near future. This was a strategy that would surprise no one, for the company had done so in the past—witness the Silver Cloud III/Silver Shadow introductions.

Significant modifications had been made to the cars, at any rate. An automatic ride control system was the most remarkable acheivement.

Accelerometers measuring vertical, longitudinal, and lateral movements, along with road surface conditions and braking and steering inputs, fed all of this data into a control unit, which compared the inputs with programmed threshold values and adjusted shock values almost instantaneously. Both roadholding and comfort benefited from this technology, and eliminated the need for a multiple–setting ride comfort switching system, as found on other cars.

The cars also benefited from a lower unsprung weight, thanks to new 15–spoke alloy wheels, which were standard.

Inside, the fruits of an extensive ergonomics research program had been realized. The dashboard had been redesigned, with many controls and switches repositioned. A new warning module, positioned directly in the driver's field of vision, provided information on vital systems and fluids as needed.

The bi–level air–conditioning system received two additional dashboard outlets. The entertainment system had 10 speakers and was considered to provide concert hall–quality sound. The front seats were electrically heated and had electrically operated lumbar supports. There was also a new, two–spoked, leather–trimmed steering wheel. Walnut veneers were complemented by boxwood inlays and crossbanding.

The going–away view of a 1983 Bentley Mulsanne Turbo. This was the car that re–established Bentley as a worthy marque in its own right.

The rear seats were electronically adjustable, and the center armrest housed a socket for a cellular telephone.

Both cars were powered by the familiar 6.75–liter V–8. Fuel management was provided by a K–Motronic fuel injection system. All four–door cars now had automatic ride control. For the first time, an anti–theft alarm was standard.

The Silver Spirit II remained in production through 1996, at which time it was replaced by the current Silver Dawn. The Silver Spur II ceased production in 1995; its role in the lineup is now occupied by the Silver Seraph, in production since 1998. As for Bentley, its performance lineup also included the Azure of 1995–97, and the current Bentley Arnage, in production since 1998.

The Silver Seraph is the first all–new Rolls–Royce in almost twenty years. It is available in a single trim level, and feature dual airbags with an occupant–sensing system, antilock brakes, traction control, and an inertial sensor that unlocks the doors and shuts off the fuel in the event of an accident.

Under the hood is a new 5.4–liter V–12 engine, developed in conjunction with BMW, linked to a five–speed automatic transmission The engine is rated at 322 hp; Rolls broke with tradition and announced the horsepower rating as the engine is essentially the same as that powering top–end BMW products.

Luxury appointments include Connolly leather, Wilton carpeting, tulip wood trim, heated power front and rear seats with lumbar support, and an Alpine AM/FM stereo system with a 6–CD, console–mounted changer and remote control for rear–seat passengers. The car lists for approximately $216,000 as of this writing.

The new Bentley Arnage is named for a famous curve at the LeMans race circuit where Bentley first gained the world's attention. The four–door saloon is powered by a BMW–engineered 4.5–liter V–8 that provides 350 hp. It boasts a pair of water–cooled turbochargers provided by the race technology group at Cosworth Engineering, itself recently acquired by BMW.

The car has a governed top speed of 150 mph and can do the zero–to–60 mph test in only 6.2 seconds. Power is smoothly brought to the road by a five–speed adaptive transmission, and there is an all–new suspension system that automatically adjusts to both road and driver inputs to give an optimal balance between ride and handling, ensuring dynamic balance in all driving conditions.

Bringing it all to a stop is a new, four–channel antilock braking system that utilizes automatic stability control to maintain composure, and ventilated disk brakes to reel the big car in, which it can do from 60 mph in just 3 seconds, or within 42 meters (140 feet) of road.

A 1997 Bentley Continental. Amidst the aerodynamic body cladding, its radiator and headlights only hint at its heritage.

The Future

Rolls–Royce, when unloaded by Vickers, was subjected to the most incredible juggling act in the history of corporate takeovers. BMW had long sought the company, and had already made investments in its engine technology in a joint venture. It was a sale Vickers wanted to make, but shareholder pressure caused it to capitulate to a larger bid from Volkswagen. BMW executives were aghast, but not so much as the Volkswagen contingent, when it discovered its premium purchase price did not provide it with the rights to produce Rolls–Royce motor cars beyond the year 2002. In the meantime, Volkswagen has rationalized the circumstances to itself, pronouncing itself totally satisfied with the opportunity to develop the Bentley marque, which it feels is a better match of the two. It has also pledged careful stewardship of Rolls–Royce until it hands over the company to its German rival, although what this means in interim product development cannot be told.

And yes, Volkswagen is happy with its Bentley purchase. The acquisition positions VW as a total carmaker (now comprising Bentley, Porsche, Audi, VW and Seat) with highly diversified lines, and the Bentley acquisition gives the conglomerate some much–sought status. Both Bentley and VW have established reputations in powerplant engineering, and VW is applying some of its trickiest designs to future Bentley platforms. One, the Hunaudiere (named after yet another section of the LeMans circuit) is a rolling laboratory for a W–16 engine (think two banks of eight cylinders, each being two staggered banks of four) that it promises will power future Bentleys, including a future LeMans contender.

British they may no longer be, but Rolls–Royce and Bentley live on.

The "Spirit of Ecstasy" hood ornament, adorning a 1972 Rolls. Rarely have a trademark and the car it represents been so tightly entwined in the public's mind.